# The Fourth Wise Ma1

By Chris Sn

Drawings by Bud

*To Gordon - This one's for you with my love.*
*You're never far from my thoughts.*

First Published in September 1991 by
QUAY BOOKS EXETER.
Tuck Mill Cottage,
Payhembury, Nr Honiton.
DEVON. EX 14 OHF.
Tel. 0404 84 388.

Copies of the musical script and demonstration tape of
THE FOURTH WISE MAN
by Chris Smith, with original music by Keith Vaughan
(available by writing to the publishers.)

Designed by Laurence Daeche, Anonymous Design Company, Exeter
Printed by Phillips & Co, Crediton

ou know how when you are waiting for something good to happen, something that you have been looking forward to, something exciting, time seems to drag. It can never come soon enough - like Christmas - well, Syllabub felt exactly like this about his birthday.

Who's Syllabub ? The Fourth Wise Man of course, but then I'm starting at the end of my tale, let me go back to the beginning.

n a time and a land far off, many years ago there lived a King called Syllabub. He was kind and he was wise, but if he had any fault at all it was perhaps that he spent too much time locked away in his splendid palace and had little contact with the people of his kingdom. If the land that he ruled was a little remote, then so too was King Syllabub from his loyal countrymen and women.

1

Syllabub's kingdom stretched as far as the eye could
see in every direction, but like everything it had a
beginning and an end and he counted as neighbours
other wise Kings such as Melchior, Balthasar and
Casper and rulers like Emperor Augustus Caesar. So
as to be certain of how many people lived in his
Empire, Caesar decreed that everybody should report
to their nearest large town, on a certain day, and
register their names. Then having compiled a list of all
his citizens, he would be able to set the taxes
accordingly.

In one corner of his Empire there lived a humble
carpenter and his wife Mary and when the order to
register came, although she was expecting a baby at
any moment, they set off to the town of Bethlehem. At
the same time Syllabub was preparing to celebrate his
birthday and was sending out invitations to a grand
party for his friends and neighbours, the other Wise Men.

Mary and Joseph's journey to Bethlehem was fairly
uneventful, although they couldn't travel as fast as
they might have liked due to Mary's condition. But
eventually they arrived.

Due to the numbers of people who had come to
register their names, and because of the fact that
Joseph hadn't thought to book a room before they left
home, they couldn't find anywhere to stay. They were
both desperately tired and needed somewhere to rest
their weary heads after the long journey to Bethlehem.
But, as fortune fell, a kind Innkeeper took one look at
Mary and offered to let them rest in a stable round
the back of his Inn. Gratefully they accepted.

eanwhile on a hillside overlooking the town, three shepherds were also trying to get some rest. The night was bitterly cold and the wind whistled across the hills, making a low moaning sound punctuated only by the occasional bleat from a new born lamb. Below them the lights of Bethlehem twinkled like a thousand glow worms which one by one were being extinguished. Above them the sky was clear and cloudless and the stars shone down as if someone had cast a handfull of silver gems into the dark night.

It was the lambing season and the shepherds were looking after their masters' flocks, helping out any ewe who was having difficulty but most important keeping a sharp eye out for any fox who chanced along and decided that here was a ready made meal just for the taking.

They had been passing the time with a friendly game of cards before huddling together under their thick warm blankets and trying to get some sleep. Jack, one of the shepherds, was about to drop off when the sky around them seemed to grow lighter. If he didn't know better he would have thought that dawn was breaking, but it was far too early for he knew that morning wouldn't come for many long hours yet.

As he roused himself, so too did the other shepherds and they found themselves bathed in a warm golden light, as if summer had come again to that hillside above the town.

From within the middle of the glow, from out of its very centre, a figure appeared. It shone with an incandescent brilliance and to look directly at it hurt Jack's eyes. He and the others were suddenly very frightened.

The invitations had gone out. Not a large list, but Syllabub's closest and nearest friends. Melchior, Balthasar and Casper would be here soon. What a feast he had in store for them. What a party he had planned. There'd be stacks of food from turkish delight to dates, figs and stuffed olives, kebabs and bread to sweetmeats and cream. There'd be gallons of wine, from the pine scented retsina to the full bodied ruby red dessert wines. He had arranged singing and dancing and at the end of the evening he knew that they would all settle down around the blazing log fire to swop stories and yarns far into the night

At the table laden with Syllabub's finest silver and gold, his cook and butler were putting the finishing touches to their master's banquet table. They knew what a big occasion this was to be and they wanted everything to be just right. The cook had been putting in hours of overtime. The pantry boy had been run off his feet. The butler had spent days shining up the royal silver and now the time had almost arrived. The party would begin in just a little while. Everything was in place and all that was needed now was the arrival of the birthday party guests.

Upstairs Syllabub had soaked in a bath brimfull of hot steaming water, frothy with a blend of aromatic oils and now he was dressing in his finest robes ready to greet his friends.

ack on the hillside outside Bethlehem, there came news of another birthday. The shepherds were just about able to distinguish the white shape burning brightly in the midst of the glow when a voice spoke to them.

" Don't be frightened " it said. " I bring you news that will make the whole world dance and sing. Tonight in a stable behind an Inn in Bethlehem is born a new King and he will be called Jesus."

" How will we know him ? " asked Jack, who was a little bit bolder than the rest. " How will we find him ? "

" Look for the brightest star in the night sky and there under that guiding beacon light, you will find the new baby King, laying in a crib surrounded by animals and watched over by his loving mother Mary with proud Joseph standing by."

" I don't believe this ".

The vision started to fade. " I don't believe this," repeated Jack. " A new King ? "

As the light started to dim the voice came again, more faintly this time. " A new King, who has come to save the world."

As quickly as it had come, the light had faded and the three shepherds once again found themselves surrounded by the dark inky night.

" Did you see what I saw ? "

" Did you hear what I heard ?"

" Pinch me. I must be dreaming."

" Dream or no, it's not my imagination  seeing that." The other two shepherds turned to look in the direction that Jack was pointing. High above the town, now almost in total darkness, there shone a star which stood out from all the others in the sky that night for it shone more brightly. No matter how long and hard you looked at it, the star  remained constant, unchanging, unblinking exactly as the message had foretold. This must be the star that marked the birthplace. The star that heralded the birth of a new King.

"Come on," said Jack, "we're going to a birthday party!"

As I said, it's terrible waiting for something nice to happen, especially if it's waiting for your own birthday party to start.

Syllabub could hardly bear it. His anxiety rubbed off on the cook and butler although they had more than enough to occupy them getting ready to take their minds off the waiting.

" It's a bit like a watched kettle sire, " said the Butler.

" *What is ?* " " It never boils " " *What doesn't ?* "

" A kettle " " *What are you talking about ?* "

" Waiting for something." " *What on earth has that got to do with a kettle ?* "

" Well you know the old saying ? A watched kettle never boils." " *You mean like an early bird catches the worm ?* "

" If you like yes." " *But they're not early. They're distinctly late.* "

At that moment Syllabub heard  camels arriving in the in the courtyard below. He rushed to the window.

" They're here, " he exclaimed. " At last, they're here ! "

" I'll go and let them in then," said the Butler, somewhat put out as he'd lost the chance to explain to Syllabub about his  watched kettle theory. Another time perhaps, when the King was less distracted.

The three Kings dismounted and handed the reins of their camels to the waiting grooms.Then, reaching up to the packs, set high up on the camels' backs behind

the saddles they each got out the birthday presents
that they had brought Syllabub. The finely dressed
Kings had brought him something special to mark his
birthday and they had just finished unpacking when
the Butler arrived to conduct them up the turret steps
into the grand ballroom.

" If you'd like to follow me, your majesties ? " as he led
the way across the court yard, lit by flaming torches,
towards the winding staircase.

Two floors above, Syllabub's excitement had reached
bursting point. He practically ran across the room and
tugged hard on the bell rope so as to summon the cook
to serve drinks to his guests.

As he did so, and the bell tinkled in the kitchen far
below in the basement, the great wooden door swung
open and the Butler stepped into the room.

" Please welcome King Balthasar who brings you a gift
of fabulous frankincense."
Balthasar moved forward. " My old friend. It is so good
to see you again after all this time. May I be the first
to wish you many happy returns of the day ? Please
accept this as a token of my fondest regard for you."

Syllabub took the offered gift and embraced his friend.

" You are welcome to my humble home "

" Now greet King Melchior," continued the Butler,
" who carries a gift of marvellous myrrh."

Melchior bowed low. " It is both my honour and my
privilege to join you and your friends on this most
illustrious of occasions and I wish you much joy and
hope that you will take my little gift to celebrate your
birthday."

Syllabub blushed with pleasure as he helped his guest
to his feet. " You are doubly welcome to my palace."

The Butler cleared his throat. " And last but by no
means least, welcome kind King Casper who brings
that most treasured of gifts, gold."

" Syllabub, more treasured than the precious metal
that I carry is my friendship and my regard for you,
your and my old friends. It is an honour to be asked to

break bread at your table and toast you with a draft of your wine. Long life, much happiness and good health my friend."

Syllabub was almost overcome with emotion and swallowed hard before replying.

" You are thrice welcome. You are all welcome here. It is my honour to have such worthy friends as you. You all do me a great service by sharing this occasion with me tonight. Come, bring on the wine, let's eat, drink and be merry for we have much to celebrate."

**H**ow different the scene that the shepherds found when they arrived in Bethlehem. Sure enough the birth place of the new baby was much as the vision's voice had described, but somehow a poor stable seemed the wrong sort of place in which to find a new born King.

**B**ack in Syllabub's palace the party was in full swing. There was much laughter and merry making and a great deal of hard work for the cook and the butler. They hardly had the time to catch their breath  so busy were they keeping the wine jugs full and keeping pace with the washing up. There was no doubt at all that the party was a great, great success and that all the Wise Men were having a wonderful time.

The dancing and entertainment over, just before they settled down for the part of the evening that Syllabub had most been looking forward to, the story telling and swopping of tales round the fire, he clapped his hands for silence.

" My friends, " he said " I have had a most delightful
evening in your company and I am deeply touched by
your kind presents to celebrate my birthday. I thank
you all most sincerely. We must all get together again
in the very near future. And, talking of the future let
us now hear from the court astrologer. Summon
Tamara."

Tamara was a local gipsy and for many years she had
been gazing into her crystal ball and foretelling the
future for Syllabub. He was not sure that he entirely
believed all that she told him, but at the very least it
was a bit of harmless fun.

Tamara appeared and sat opposite the end of the great
dining table, now practically cleared of food. She
hunched over her  glass ball and her eyes began to
mist over and become somehow sort of vacant.

" The glass is beginning to clear. I can see a stable in a land far from here where a mother has just laid her new born baby in a crib of hay. This is no ordinary baby though, he is a New King. The Lord of all Mankind."

Syllabub practically exploded. " The Lord of all Mankind ? "

The other Kings became very excited too.

" A new king ? "

" This we must see."

" How do we find him ? "

Unhurried and unflustered by all the excitement she had generated around her, the Gipsy Queen continued.

" Find the brightest star in the night sky and follow this to the East. There you will find the new King surrounded by animals in a cattle stall under the star."

King Casper leapt to his feet no longer able to contain himself.

" Come on !! Let's go !! "

Casper was almost out of the door as the ever reasonable and practical Balthasar halted him in his tracks.

" Hang on ! We have no birthday presents for him."


In that instant the bottom fell out of their world. It
was Syllabub who restored things to an even keel and
came to the rescue with a brilliant idea.

" You can take the ones that you bought me."
Casper grasped this solution to the problem in an
instant.

" I thank you."

" We all thank you," added Melchior. " But what about
you ? Aren't you coming ? "

" Me ? Why yes, of course. But you go on without me.
Your camels are already saddled for the journey. I have
to make mine ready, prepare and pack for the trip and
I shall have to find a present fit for a King."

" A box of your finest jewels would make a great gift, "
suggested Balthasar.


Leaving Syllabub to consider this, the Kings set off. As
he left the room, Melchior turned back.

" Syllabub. Thank you for the evening. Follow as soon
as you can."

" I won't be far behind, I promise. Farewell. Be on your
way."

They embraced and held each other close, then Melchior was gone, following the others.

The Fourth Wise Man was left alone.

" Harness my camel. Pack my saddle bags. Look out my warm cloak. Select a box of my finest jewels. I am on my way to meet the Lord of all Mankind."

he Shepherds gazed in silence at the new baby, hardly daring to speak or even breathe for fear of disturbing the sleeping child. Mary, his mother, seemed to be asleep and barely noticed their presence although at one time she did raise her head from her chest, look up at the three shepherds and smile. Joseph had thanked them for coming although no thanks were needed, George, Sam and Jack would not have missed this for the world.

" At least I can say to my children that I was there, " whispered Jack.

" Have you noticed, " muttered Sam in reply " how all the animals seem to know that this is a special occasion and are standing with their heads bowed low in the presence of the new born King."

" It's magic, " said George.

" Whatever it is," replied Sam, " it's wonderful."

he other Kings had got a head start by the time that Syllabub was out of the Palace and onto the road to follow after them. Before many hours had passed night began to fall and there was still no sign of his friends.

" The others are probably there by now. I don't like it by myself. It's cold, it's dark and it's lonely and they say that robbers and outlaws live in these woods that I am passing through. Oh, I wish that I was at home again in front a nice warm fire. "

Syllabub, saddle sore and very weary now was leading his camel as dusk grew into darkest night. A shrieking owl startled him and if truth were told he was now very frightened indeed. What had seemed like a good idea and something of an adventure within the warm confines of his palace, full of fine food and drink, had lost all of its appeal and he now truely wished himself anywhere but where he was.

" I must journey on and be brave. I must follow that star."

Suddenly without any warning at all Syllabub felt a hand upon his shoulder. An evil sounding  voice hissed in his ear.

" Don't turn around, just hand over that box that
you're carrying."

" But there's nothing in it to interest you," said
Syllabub shaking like a leaf.

" I'll be the judge of that. Hand it over !"

As he passed the box over his shoulder to the man
behind him Syllabub let go of the reins to his camel.
The animal sensing that all was far from well, took off
at a tremendous gallop and disappeared, crashing
through the trees.

Syllabub turned around slowly and faced the man who
had taken from him his birthday gift for the new born
King as he was opening the small chest brimfull of
gold and silver jewels.

Although the darkness made it difficult to see him, it
was clear that he had fallen upon hard times.

" Why ? Why are you doing this ? Why take from me my present for the New Born King ? " demanded Syllabub.

" Why ? Do you know what it is to be hungry and cold ? To have no-where to call your own to lay your head at the end of the day ? You look like a fine man who probably has a nice warm home. Whose family want for nothing."

' I have no family ' thought Syllabub, ' unless you count the subjects in my kingdom.'

" When my children look at me," continued the robber, " it's not love that I see in their eyes but a great big question. Why us ? Why do we have to eat so little when others have so much ? Why do we have no food in our stomachs when others are so fat ? Why are we so cold when others are so snug and warm ? They are questions that I cannot answer ".

" But this is no solution surely. Robbing people. How did you become an outlaw ? "

" I became unemployed and could not find work. Having lost my job, I lost my home and so we had to come and live in these woods. This has become the only way I know of getting money."

" I'm sorry."

" I don't want your sympathy. I have all of yours that I want."

" You mean the jewels ? You are welcome to them.
Have them, with my blessing."

" You don't mind ? "

" Only in as much as they were intended as a present
for the new King born in Bethlehem, but your need is
greater than either mine or his. I meant that I was
sorry that I had lived for so long in my palace shut off
from the world, unaware of how people were having to
live in my Kingdom and how hard it was to earn your
keep. You have opened my eyes, and for that I am
grateful."

" But it is I who should thank you."

" Think no more of it. Now be off with you before I
change my mind."

The robber stared at Syllabub long and hard. " I don't
really understand."

" Nor did I, my friend. Nor did I. Be off and give my
regards to your wife and family."

" I will sir. God bless you."

" And you too." And as silently as he had come the
robber melted back into the woods and in a moment he
was gone.

 Syllabub pulled his fine warm cloak tighter around
himself, " I must travel  on, " he said looking up at the
star burning brightly in the  dark sky away to  the
East.........

*Away in a manger*
*No crib for his bed*
*The little Lord Jesus*
*Lay down his sweet head......*

The night grew colder as Syllabub, now on foot,
plodded his weary way and he began to
question the wisdom of making this journey.
It looked as if his friends were miles in front of him
and now without his camel, which he hadn't seen since
it went careering into the woods, he started to wonder
if he'd ever arrive. The star seemed further away than
ever.

When morning broke, along with it came one of those
damp swirling mists which seemed to creep into the
very marrow of the bones and his thick cloak provided
little protection.

As the mist began to clear, ahead of him in the road,
Syllabub saw a shuffling figure coming towards him.
As the person came closer he saw that it was a woman,
bent low against a long, white stick. She however
didn't seem to realise that he was approaching her
until they almost bumped into each other.

23

" Who goes there ? " she called out in alarm.

" Only a fellow traveller, " Syllabub replied.

" Where are you going ? "

" I have heard tell of the birth of a new King in a town far from here called Bethlehem. I am on my way to see him."

" Alas, " said the woman, " that is something that I will never be able to do, for my eyes are covered with a veil of darkness. For me day is always night and the sun never shines. Although I can feel the warmth on my face, its rays can never penetrate my heart."

Syllabub realised that she was blind. " But is there nothing that can be done to restore your sight ? Can no one help ? "

" It is said that in Jerusalem there are doctors who have the skill necessary "

" Then what stops you from going ? "

" The money,"replied the blind woman with a simplicity that almost broke Syllabub's heart. " The money that it costs good sir."

He thought for a split second and then quite spontaneously took off his fine gold crown, encrusted with sparkling jewels and held it out to her. " Here, take this."

She took it cautiously in her hands. " I am unable to see what it is that you have given me, but I can tell by its feel and weight that it is something of value, but why ? Why choose me ? "

Syllabub shrugged. " In a way it is you that have chosen me. You have made me realise that it is I who have been blind. You have opened my eyes. You have made ME see. I who had everything, never gave a thought for those that had nothing. Now my eyes have been opened and I can see dimly, but more clearly."

The blind woman, were she able, would have wept tears of happiness. She leaned towards Syllabub and gently kissed him on the cheek. " You sir have a heart of gold. God bless you. "

" God bless you too " he replied.......

*The stars in the bright sky*
*Looked down where he lay*
*The little Lord Jesus*
*Asleep in the hay.*

The mid-day sun had burned off the last of the early morning mist and Syllabub could feel its searing heat upon his neck. He still wore his cloak with the collar turned up for protection against the scorching rays. ' It surely cannot be much further ' he thought to himself. By now though he had realised that his journey did have purpose and a meaning and that even if he never got to see the new King, the trip had been infinitely worthwhile. His thoughts were interrupted by a voice from the road-side.

" Can you help me sir ? "

Turning, he looked down to see a hunched up beggar squatting in the ditch along the dusty track.

" What has happened to you ? "

The man stood as if in reply and began to tell his story.

" I was a farmer who fell upon hard times. A plague of locusts ravaged my crops and there followed a long summer drought. My cattle died and because the grain harvest had failed I had no money to buy more. I put my farm up for sale, but because everybody was in the same boat as me, it fetched next to nothing at auction. I just had enough to pay off my debts and was left with little to live on. I took to travelling the roads and trying to scrape a living as best I could. I'm tired and hungry and the nights are so cold. Please help me."

Syllabub took off the cloak from his back and handed it to the poor farmer. " It is not in my power to do much more than to help you to keep warm at night. I too have no money but you are welcome to this cloak. You will find if you examine it closely that the buttons are made of gold, that the thick  chain which fastens it at the throat is solid silver and the weights at the bottom which make it hang down are large emeralds. Perhaps you would be wise to find a buyer for it and maybe the proceeds will help set you on your feet again. "

As Syllabub had been talking, the poor farmer's mouth had dropped open in disbelief. He shook his head slowly, unable to take in what Syllabub offered.

" Many have passed me by without giving so much as a backward glance. Why did you stop ? "

" I have learned on my journey not to judge men nor women by their outward appearances. Besides, there is much joy in giving."

" And in receiving," said the farmer. " I thank you for your kindness and I wish you Godspeed on your voyage."

The farmer bowed to kiss Syllabub's hand.

" That is not necessary. Your thanks are enough."

As night fell, Syllabub arrived on the outskirts of Bethlehem. The star was now shining almost directly overhead and he realised that he was near his journey's end. ' I've made it. I'm here.' he almost shouted out loud. " Excuse me," he said stopping someone passing by,

" Can you show me which way to the stable where I will find the new born King ? "

" That will be the Three Crowns that you're after I expect. I've had a lot of people stopping me to find the way there, shepherds, Kings, all sorts."

' They are already here ' thought Syllabub, delighted to have some news of his friends.

" Up here, turn left at the top and then first right. The Three Crowns Inn is down there on the right. You can't miss it. "

" I thank you kind sir, " Syllabub said as he went hurrying off up the road as instructed. Having turned left, he then took the first turning on the right into a narrow side street and there, sure enough, was the Inn that he was seeking. More than that, just ahead of him in the street coming from the opposite direction, down the cobbled road were the three other Kings, Casper, Melchior and Balthasar.

" My friends, " he shouted. " It's me! I'm here! I've
arrived!"

The Kings steadfastly ignored him as they turned into
the alleyway next to the Inn, making their way round
the back to the stable.

" Casper ! Melchior ! Balthasar ! It's me ! " They moved
in through the stable door without turning toward
him. ' They don't recognise me without my crown, my
robe or my kingly apparell.'

Ⅱnside the stable the Kings presented the new
baby with their gifts. Joseph thanked them most
warmly.

Syllabub was about to rush in when he suddenly
stopped in his tracks, halted by a thought that had
come  into his head from no-where.

' I  have no present for the new King. I cannot go in. I
have nothing to give him.' His heart felt like lead and
a great sadness swept over him.

Then,  in the darkness outside the stable a bright light
filled the sky. The light burned fiercely and shone so
brightly that Syllabub had to shield his eyes.

" I have nothing to give him " Syllabub repeated aloud.

In reply, from within the centre of the light came a
voice, the voice of an angel.

" Syllabub it is enough that you brought yourself. The baby King is sleeping soundly at present. His mother Mary laying by his side with proud Joseph standing watch. Next to the crib are fabulous gifts. The baby has been visited by both the meek and the powerful, but you are welcome here to join with them in their birthday celebrations after your long and eventful journey."

Syllabub remained unconvinced, uncertain about going in.

" But I told you, I have nothing to give him."

" Except yourself. Except yourself."

The light began to fade and  darkness fell again. The angel's words echoed in Syllabub's ears and suddenly he understood. Drawing himself to his feet, having fallen to his knees as the angel appeared, he moved towards the stable door, slowly at first and then with more confidence.

Pushing open the door it was all as the angel had described.

Mother and baby with the father looking over them, the shepherds and the animals and the most recent arrivals, the three Wise Men. Now, however, they were joined by another King, Syllabub. The Fourth Wise Man had arrived.